I0483979

Enter

The Game Business

Copyrights © 2015 Sam iy

ISBN-10: 1511601663

ISBN-13: 978-1511601665

Dedication

To all of you wishing to enter the game production
industry and be part of the exciting game world!.
Enjoy making games that come to life by bringing it to the
user in form of "play with fun".
If you wonder how you can join the mass of game makers
then this is for you to get quickly on your feet starting
your own game business in no time, it gives you the
information you need to get started, the right tools to use,
and takes your worries away.
No more waisting time hesitating and being afraid.
If you wish to just try the game business before making
a decision to switch jobs this is for you, and if you love to
make your switch now this is as well for you.
It is easy and simple, the choice is of course yours!

Table Of Contents:

1. Introduction

2. Game Business

3. Game Industry Positions

4. The Designer and The Tools

4.1 The Designer

4.2 The Designer's Tools

5. The Artist and the Tools

5.1 The Artist

5.2 The Artist's Tools

5.2.1 2D Tools

5.2.2 3D Tools

6. The Developer and the Tools

6.1 The Developer

6.2 The Developer's Tools

7. Game Making Elements

7.1 Hardware

7.2 Software

8. Art Creation

9. Game Engines

10. Popular Software

11. Starting The Business

12. Advantage of Owning a Company

13. Project Scope and Size

14. Test the Game

15. Team Organization

15.1 The Waterfall method

15.2 Agile development method

15.3 Version Control method

15.4 Iterative method

16. GitHub

17. Game Assets

17.1 3D Assets

17.1.1 Rendering to texture

17.1.2 Texture Mapping

17.1.3 Polygon

17.1.4 Animations

17.2 2D Assets

17.2.1 Pixels

17.2.2 Hitboxes

18. Sound effect

19. Buying Assets Option

20. Hiring Someone

21. Ask Yourself

22. Making money out of Games

22.1 Overview

22.2 Premium Games Characteristics

22.3 Freemium Games Characteristics

23. Ways to make money with free Games

23.1 In App Purchases

23.2 In game advertising

23.3 IGA

23.4 Online games Advertisement

23.5 Pay to Play

24. Targeted Audience

25. Game Statistics

26. Helping the user

27. Risks and Challenges

28. Things To Consider

29. Conclusion

1. Introduction:

When this industry started it was very different than today's way, why? Simply because of the evolution of the tools that we use nowadays from game consoles, home computers that are gone away basically, the fact that we used to spend a lot's of money to buy a console game to play at home.

That's being said not many games were produced and we had to wait for the next year's game to come out.
Why? Because few companies where making games so there were not many of them out there.
The discs were physically printed, plus the shipping time and the effort to get them out to the stores then getting to put them on shelf to sell them for a period of time.
Some game developers had to burn their own discs to ship them and sell them and that was time consuming.
Now with the digital world it got much easier to produce and distribute games, by simply making it available online anyone and anywhere in the world it can be downloaded .
therefore it is exposed to millions of people in less time and the rarity is gone.
Even old games are easily downloadable online.
Also the mobile, tablets and other smart devices marketed and facilitated that as well not just the online side.
Everyone can play games on mobile devices and millions of people have a smart phone and to pass time while riding a bus or waiting for it they just jump on playing games, while in the past it was limited access.

You need just to choose to play the game you're interested in and voila! You're in.

Even in Airplanes people once allowed they grab their phones and start playing.

Games-apps are huge in the smart phones and tablets market, simply because you are free to play them anywhere from the confort of your home or outside you're not stuck in one spot or obligated to be in a specific place to have fun playing games anymore.

Also things got cheaper than the traditional console game and even many of them are free nowadays you don't have to pay anything to be able to access them.

2. Game Business:

The methods of doing business changed from premium experience where when you pay for the game you own it, occasionally free ones are out there to get without paying, to share and possibly buy in the future.

Now we have the free premium that makes money with games, so you get it for free with an option to pay for an upgrade. But what changed? The number of Indie games developers is growing, more than ever, after the game industry flourished those small companies with few developers grew big, and the digital world offers an opportunity to everyone to make a game and expose it to the world, being indie doesn't mean small at all, in fact you can make millions of dollars from it seen in many cases once released in major platforms.

I encourage you to be an indie game developer! It is exciting and very interesting.

No matter where you want to be working be part of a team that enjoys doing it, build a great resume to amaze your boss by having a game even a small one, Just to give a proof of your ability to produce and release a game.

All what you need is really the desire to be part of this industry.

Do you enjoy it? Then why not participate.

Do you think it is hard? That's why you're afraid to do it...well if this is the case then think again because it is very easy!!!.

3. Game Industry Positions:

Well to make a game gather a team that you believe is capable to deliver the product, So you definitely need and must have an artist, a developer and a designer and you may choose to have more than the three essentials which is optional.

So it is not limited to the three above specially in the section of marketing by getting a marketer that gets the game out there to sell well and be exposed to the world in no time, and you may have a sponsor that pays for the whole production of the game why not if you don't have the finance for it get help if your game is huge.

So if you decide to start you really need a design based on an idea, the art then you need to develop the idea and take it to a higher level. Without those three it will not work.

An artist for example is needed to make the design visual for people to see.

Saying all that I don't mean that you need three people to do it, if yourself are able to do the three part roles then be it! What I meant is the main roles are those three then comes other sub-roles that can be added.

4. The Designer and The Tools:

4.1. The Designer:

The designer is the thinker of all the parts that will make the game, it is not as easy as you might think, it is not about just writing down the ideas or the story as a whole, but instead he/she details every part and inch of the story.

Do you still think of the designer as doing nothing? He/She puts the pieces together and if there are characters that talk the designer is the one to write their dialogues, takes care of the levels, the type of characters, so it is really more than writing, there are so many details and events going on in the story game.

Let's say it is a shooting game then he/she has to go beyond the characters and think about the types of weapons, the damage level, the healing tools and so on...the interaction with other characters, there are thought in the head of the designer put on a paper detailing every aspect of the game, not easy at all to do. The designer is the inventor of the game, it is in his/her head and he/she has to communicate that to others, therefore explaining the details to the team to follow the vision to make it happen.

4.2. The Designer's Tools:

Excel:
Is the designer's favorite tool, because he/she needs to make spreadsheets, a very common tool to put the specific ideas similar to a blank canvas used by the painting artist where it becomes his/hers.

Word document:
Is also commonly used to write the ideas and details, a language skill is needed and very important.
A designer also does a lot of math with the choice to give it to the developer.

5. The Artist and the Tools:

5.1 The Artist:
Considering that there are many types of artists that create 2D and 3D art, we are not pointing to the oil painting artists, but we can include the musicians, in fact it is related to what you see and hear in a game, and the artist is needed to create this part, he/she looks after the look of items and characters, backgrounds and scenes, and many other things to take care of...in bigger companies artists are focused on one task at the time but in indie one person can be multitasking and that depends on how big the project is and the type of art if it is 2D then it does not need a 3D artist, also if the game includes sounds and music or none...

In huge games the artist is a big part of the development, companies hire as many as needed to meet the deadline production, each will be required to achieve a specific task then in the end all the pieces will be gathered to make one whole piece, from animating characters to just sounds effects, in the end once joined make the game.

5.2 The Artist's Tools:
Because of the specific task of each artist there are specific tools as well to choose from and the widely used ones are:

5.2.1 2D Tools:

Photoshop:
A raster type making and editing images software with *.PSD* default file extension, developed by Adobe Systems, the best editing tool to draw, also edits 3D graphics that used to be done through plug-ins, which still offer expansion to the software
The software cost money to buy it but it delivers the best art work, and is considered by far the best and favorite tool of developers and artists, the software comes with a free trial.

Gimp:
A free raster software meaning a rectangular grid of points, a software where the image is characterized by the width and hight, it retouches and edits the image, converts the file to many different formats, crops and resizes images, and much more.

Note:
you can improve its functionality by adding plug-ins.
It does almost similar work as Photoshop.

Pixlr:
Can be used in a web browser without the need to install it, helps make quick fixes, adds effects and cool transformations to photos, it works online and offline.
It all comes to your preferences and which tools you like the best based on your needs and the type of game you're creating.
You can use the free version which is good enough to help you get the work done, the membership option has more features but you have to pay a fee.

5.2.2 3D Tools:

Maya:
it does all what the artist needs to make a good product, from animation and simulation to rendring, it delivers high quality work and comes with a free trial.

3ds Max:
Widely used in games, TV, Films, helps create assets quickly saving you time, helps you focus on creativity offering high technical tools to create and animate characters fast with powerful iterations and choices when rendering images, and comes with a free trial.

Note:

Blender is a free 3D modeling and animation software, it can be used instead of Maya and 3ds Max if you are a beginner, train yourself using this tool once getting good at 3D, then you can decide for yourself to buy or not the payed versions of Maya and 3ds Max as their quality production is amazing.

6. The Developer and the Tools:

6.1 The Developer:

After the designer's idea and the artist's assets comes the developer he/she is the one that collects the pieces and makes it as a one piece to make it alive, the game is not anymore on paper or in section of art work but a whole thing with coding to make it interactive and interesting.

It is by programming and getting the computer to execute tasks needed for the game to come alive. But we still use developer instead of programmer because some games don't need programming to come alive.

AI is very difficult to do and is a specific task, which is based on the artificial intelligence used to make intelligent behaviors, but in games it includes control, robotics computer science techniques within environment limitations.

Sometimes tricks are used to make the AI smarter than it is by the developer which makes people think that it is very smart by giving the game a way to send an info beyond the limited frame.

The designer and developer can work together as a team to clarify things and characters and other details, they are really two distinct roles which doesn't mean two persons necessarily, it is just that one comes with the idea and the other executes it to make it come alive.

6.2 The Developer's tools:

Notepad:

Free and simple text editor, with **.txt** extension file, used for coding sometimes, fast loading, very basic text manipulation, has Find and Replace option, Font, Font style and size through Format menu, also you can add time/date from Edit menu, and create a Header/Footer through Page Setup in the File menu.

Notepad++:

Free text and code editor software, different from Notepad as it allows opening faster and working with multiple files, you can drag and drop your files directly, it allows finding and replacing, and calculates similarities and differences between files, it highlights syntax when coding.

Sublime:

Great text editor software for code , can be downloaded for free but must be purchased for continued use, the licence to buy is per user not per machine.
A cross platform software, with extending packages mostly free.

7. Game Making Elements:

7.1. Hardware:

You need a computer, any one working will do the work, but which target you try to reach? Are you interested in touch screen platform, the game target has to match the platform you use to be able to test it, if it is Xbox game then you need an Xbox, a smart phone platform might be a choice as well as millions of people own one, and works just fine as a development tool, windows phone also is another way, so you pick what you like, also the size of the screen might impact the type of games, you need to test your game on the right size to be able to analyse it and make clear decisions on details such as font size etc...

Keyboard is needed for typing, it is suggested by the developer instead of drag and drop way, also **internet** definitely is good to have.

For **3D games** you need a computer with good graphics card therefore a higher computer to run such process faster, so if you're a beginner it is better to start with something small with whatever computer you have then progress to the next levels by upgrading the tools.

Make at first a game that runs on your system without worry.

Note:

When using game engines for your 3D games get a button mouse wheel that helps you navigate.

7.2. Software:

We have two different categories of software to choose from, we have the **game engines** such as **Unity**, and the **IDE** (integrated development environment), such as Xcode for Mac Os.

8. Art Creation:

Different software available for this purpose we have 2D and 3D art.

For the 2D art, Photoshop is a payed version with a trial, but still by far the best.

We have the raster image and the vector image, Photoshop creates the raster one which is a pixel image with a resolution and a size that you can change easily to get what you need.

The vector is simply a line based picture, many use the Illustrator for this purpose where you can resize the picture without worrying about how good the **resolution** is because it is completely independent of it.

You can first create your assets as a vector type then export it to a pixel one, you want to use the pixel for the look, if you are familiar with a specific software just use it to get your work done.

For 3D most developers and companies use the 3DS Max and Maya (Autodesk) even if it is not cheap, they usually come with a free trial option or a discount which is a great way to learn the tool before investing money to buy.

9. Game Engines:

A type of software that has multiple components, and is created to design and develop video games, it has **rendering,** a graphic generator functionality for 2D and 3D pictures and movies (scene files containing defined objects), it has physics, sound, animation and the **AI** (Artificial Intelligence) which is handed to software engineers to take care of because it requires specific knowledge.

The game development can be saved and reused to create a new one for economy purposes or to ease the whole development process.

10. Popular Software:

Unity:

Great tool that goes from free to a monthly payment for the pro version with advanced features, it is a cross platform software such as web browsers, desktops, windows etc..., it also has an (IDE) integrated development environment, and the good thing is that you don't have to code from scratch because the software helps with so many parts by making the basics for you giving you the tools you need to build your game, themes are selected just with clicks.

Note:

When using Unity for your 3D games get a button mouse wheel that helps you navigate.

GameMaker:

different than Unity game engine, does the 2D version not
the 3D, it is easier to use, with a list of all the parts of
your project.

Good games have been developed with it, if you don't
know how to code than you have a drag and drop code tool
as well as the option to write a simple code by adding for
example **variables** which in programming means values
that can change based on conditions or information given
to instruct the computer, or you can use the **Scripts** which
help assign very powerful behaviours therefore a more
advanced game development.

The free version has limited features than the professional
one but to start learning the free one is good enough, it is
based on a drag and drop **(DnD)** process, it allows you to
import videos, images and sounds with instant results.

Note:

You're free to try and make your own decision on which
one is your favorite.

11. Starting The Business:

There are steps to follow when starting a business as an
indie game developer, each country has its own law and
procedures and types of business you can have.

Choose the type that you're interested in.

Sole proprietorship, in this case the company is yourself.

Corporation company, if you like the partnership type
where all involved parties sign a contract to avoid future
misunderstanding and disputes over who owns what?.

If you have a partner writing down the details in a contract form that has to be signed by all involved parties is a must! Just to avoid running in the future into serious difficult situations and problems, clarifying things on who gets what and how much of the profits is the way to proceed in this type of business, the ownership has to be stated clearly on the very important element called **IP** (intellectual property), therefore avoiding disagreements that may arise in the future.

IP: intellectual assets include inventions , software, original ideas to come-up with new product, a new way to process a method etc... They have a commercial value, meaning you can earn money from them, either commercial or tangible they offer very successful business if protected from the start, therefore avoiding any conflict with other companies trying to duplicate or make a product theirs, and gives the owner an advantage over his/her competitors.

To protect your assets you need total confidentiality then either choose to make it completely confidential or go public after issuing a **patent** that gives you the right to own the asset by submitting an application for a patent, copyright, etc...

LLC (limited liability company) found in USA, where personal assets will not be sewed.

Note:

Please consult a lawyer to find more information regarding the details of each type of business before proceeding to avoid future issues, it helps you pick the right choice if you don't have prior experience.

12. Advantage of Owning a Company:

Owning a company helps with Taxes, if you need tools to run your business, buying a computer, a console, printers etc, having a company helps you write off these equipments from your taxes.

Note:
Please check your country for taxation details.

13. Project Scope and Size:

It is necessary to define the type and size of the project in the beginning of the process of making a game, as it could be a 2D or a 3D type game.

If it is similar development of Hallo game for example, it is good to think about the amount of hours and developers needed to achieve the task, because depending on the size of the project it can end up from few to hundreds of hours to deliver the product, depending on the complexity it might need hundreds of skilled people in the field to get the work done.

Minecraft in the beginning started with one person, then when it got popular, a group of skilled people was hired to do the work as it got bigger than the start point, in this case starting as an individual was possible knowing that the computer helps generating the themes, in the other hand Hallo has more to it, and uses different approach when it comes to systems, 3D graphics, scripts and animation, a more complicated AI (artificial intelligence) programming is incorporated also the story of the game itself is very detailed, that makes this game a more complex one to make.

Simpler games can be done in no time but others using complicated mechanics can take many years to finish. Being ambitious is good but to start just try to keep it simple, build few simple game stories that help understanding the scope, the time, the cost and the labour needed to do it, this way you'll get the proper experience into knowing all the details involved during the work process therefore defining the real amount of work needed. Start small and grow from there, is the way to build the right experience.

14. Test the Game:

Get your game tested through family members or friends, having another opinion than yours is very valuable, this way you get to update your game, fix the problems and any deficiencies then again test it to ensure that users find your game appropriate and user friendly.

You can also make your game public then once popular add more features and levels to enhance the user's fun.

15. Team Organization:

15.1 The Waterfall method:

The progress moves like a waterfall in the process development software, used as a method to develop a game through principal parts organizing them in a specific order and structure such as the design, then comes the implementation, after that comes the checking and maintenance.

Developers don't like it because the game needs testing to make sure the fun is there, which is absent in this method that claims a certainty of things ahead of time without trying to discover the game's dynamism called fun.

Most contracts are made in a waterfall way, that officially order deadline for deliverables, based on illusions of certainty, to simplify explaining things to the upper management department which has people with no game development skills to understand how complex it is to do such work and therefore stick to the reality.

15.2 Agile development method:

Where the plan is based on reality to produce a game, without any illusions, it is an effective way that delivers quality understanding the complexity and the hard work process, understanding the details of making a fun game, through testing and trials, paying attention to the game mechanics.

All art, design and testing parts are balanced.

The testing is very important stage as it allows to fix, debug, update and test again until satisfaction of the fun is reached.

Based on experiences of what works and what does'nt through the balancing method which reach the quality needed before delivering the product to consumers or clients, we have a more motivated team investing efforts into producing the best because of the clear vision not illusions.

They are trusted in doing the job with more freedom that helps the creativity and functionality, the communication is great because of the small team size.

15.3 Version Control method:

A database that has all the historical data, which is good in a way it is a back-up for accidental mistakes or bad design, it offers the possibility to go back and fix things, also everyone of the team gets to work on his/her own part without stepping on other people's parts providing the latest up to date info to download and continue providing growth and progress of the game in a nice fashion, the communication this way is based on documents out in the server for others to grab and use knowing the overall progress of the product avoiding the conflict due to non communicating the changes.

A method used by bigger companies having bigger teams, therefore the source containing the code is available to designers for example looking after the art, that helps the programmer and the designer to be on the same page. Because the history is preserved, tracking down problems is easier to look at, modify then update to suit the desired quality and functionality without any problem.

Therefore this method or program allows a main line of the originale files and the new branch for the new ones. Branching allows separating the codes that are ready and by doing so the task is clear to tackle the part needing more work, bigger companies use the version control to store the assets and preserve them.

15.4 Iterative method:

Based on developing a project for a period of time then stop, and once it is ready for more features start again to work on it for some time, reaching in each step the set milestones.

Therefore the situation is in total control offering flexibility to adjust according to the progress made.

Note:
Agile methodology is the preferred one by developers, it is realistic and uses shared database same as the control version at a smaller scale, therefore facilitating the communication between the individuals of the team by updating and saving the history of the work.

16. GitHub:

Free hosting, open source projects, favored by indie developers.
It is a popular web code repository, where you can have a free or paid account, its development started in 2007, projects can be browsed, downloaded and manipulated in the public section, the site has a social networking role, and students can access tools for free to develop their projects.

17. Game Assets:

What is an asset? An asset is a useful thing similar to a benefit in general, in the game assets are the art parts that include the characters, backgrounds etc... and the sound parts such as music, sound effects, media and entertainment contents, and sometimes the human participates in the motion type game.

17.1 3D Assets:

3D stands for three dimensional space, which is in mathematical interpretation the three coordinates based on (x, y, z).

There are few things to consider:

17.1.1 Rendering to texture:

Called "texture baking" allows texture map creation based on an object and its appearance in the scene.

Textures are baked and become part of the object and can be viewed as graphics in 3D.

This process is basically recording as an image, some aspects, sims and animation are other types of "baking" it saves the rendering time and applied once to the material or Mesh once done.

It simplifies the number of texture images.

The material colors applied to texture paint can be saved to an image, it is complicated process but useful.

17.1.2 Texture Mapping:

It takes in consideration the material, the effects of lighting, the mapping and more, it adds details to the surface of the object or character.

17.1.3 Polygon:

In geometry it means a group of straight lines that close to form a circuit, when two edges meet at a point and form a corner the edges are then called vertices.

17.1.4 Animations:

Which means bringing to motion a static picture, based on consecutive pictures that create illusion of movement.

17.2 2D Assets:

There are few things to consider:

17.2.1 Pixels:

Are small squares that we cannot see when the image is displayed on the computer or as a photo print, we have three primary colors and components, the Red, the Green, and the Blue.

The digital image dimensions are measured in pixels, called pixel or resolution.

These pixels are scalable when displayed, but pixels are the same size in any digital picture.

17.2.2 Hitboxes:

Usually the animated object uses a hitbox to ensure accuracy, often found in 2D games or 3D by using a rectangle that follows a specific point on the sprite or the model.

18. Sound effect:

Audacity:

A free audio recording and editing software, it offers exporting files, also you can save the file as an Ogg (a compressed sound) used in games or WAV or MP3 for background music purpose which is a common music format, game engines come with built in support sound.

Note:

You can record your own music if you play an instrument.

19. Buying Assets Option:

Art is a skill that can be learned but is time consuming.
You can check thenounproject.com which has some assets
(icons) for free *but must credit the artist* and some others
for a fee.

Unity has its own asset store, GameMaker has its own
resources , also check TurboSquid website, it has great art
models that can be purchased and used by developers
which saves artists a lot of time.

Note:

Make sure to check the licences when your are
downloading an asset, if it is for free make sure that it
allows commercial use before incorporating it into your
game to not get in trouble.

It is greate to have access to stores to buy assets that
saves you a lot of time to draw yourself, and when the
price is reasonable why not get it right away, but it is up
to you to make the decision to make the asset or buy it, if
you decide to buy make sure that all the pieces or objects
work very good all together, it is important that things
match together otherwise check if your licence allow
switching with another more appropriate asset that works
for your game.

20. Hiring Someone:

If you feel like it is too much for you to deal with the assets and making them from start to finish or even modifying them, you can hire a specialist, an artist that makes your game stands out, with unique characters and scenes, also some art in internet are not free and you need permission to use them, think about how much money you can spend for making the game.

Social Networking:

Is a platform for people that have same interests, the user has mostly a profile and shares publicly personal information and hobbies and has a list of connections with other users, it is mostly a web based service, it is a way to share ideas, photos and more, and the most popular are **Facebook** and **Twitter**.

oDesk:(www.odesk.com)

A large online service of freelancers offering their help to those needing help in many sections from design and development to marketing and accounting, just by describing the skill you are looking for, you will find instantly someone, that you will interview then hire the strongest candidate, you can pay by project or by hour using the credit card, bank account or through payPal, without any paper work worries, a very easy and straight forward method.

Elance: (www.elance.com)
Here you post the type of work you are looking for, free of charge by describing your need you get proposals instantly from freelancers, the site also helps matching your requirements with the ones qualified through an analysis, you can check out portfolios, ratings and more to make your final decision on who to hire to do your job, the payment is protected and hassle free once satisfied with the delivered work.

Note:
When sending your request looking for someone give a description regarding your project but once you choose the qualified professional be very specific on exactly what you need to be done.
Pay attention to ratings, and pick the 5 stars if any, pick always the best, make sure you choose the right person to do your work.
To avoid any problems, make sure Not to pay in advance until the job is done, if asked to make a payment in advance make sure you pay just for the part done and so on.
Those sites have professional people, but you have to interview probably few of them before making a decision on who gets to do your work.

21. Ask Yourself:

While in the design process of the game, ask yourself about which monetization method you like to choose, it is important to do so at the beginning not at the end of the development, dont't wait and try to figure out the price at the end.

22. Making money out of Games:

22.1 Overview:

Premium, free, and freemium are the three types to monetize games, premium is the older way to buy a game software to be able to play it, or coin machines which are still used, so they are still existing and will not go away any time soon, this type can make a huge amount of money, and most games for consoles and PC's are this type.

22.2 Premium Games Characteristics:

High quality, where the expectations of users regarding the art, music and quality are taken into consideration, they come at full price that eventually drops based on contractual agreements, performance, and ratings. Premium type is not only made by large companies with high end and big budget but also by indie game makers. Big productions are called the triple A and the others are called indie, casual or independent.

So you pay up front, it is a type that has an end of content with a story, so you can complete 100% of the game.

DLC for a video game stands for Downloadable Content, through Internet, it acts as an extension or add-ons content to the game and is distributed by the official publisher or third party, DLC is used to attract users and keep them interested, this way the developers delivers a richer experience to players.

22.3 Freemium Games Characteristics:
It is a strategic way to price the game, first it is introduced free of charge, but the premium part is paid for, the game is played on the web and the mobile.
When it is free it offers an additional part to pay for to get it, you can pay for an additional character, and different type of guns and weapons that help the main character to extend health and win over the enemy for example, so the added features are priced, it is an optional offer but many users get attached to the game therefore to continue playing and winning they need to purchase more packages which they go for it!.
The so called freeware existed since the 80's, in the "lite " version offered free, for promotion purpose, in 2006 the idea of giving free service arises which comes with the premium part where you charge a fee, again you're free to buy the service or opt not to do so.
The free game downloadable type follow sometimes the same strategy for monetization purposes.
When people are hooked and in love with the game you can make a fair amount of money this way.

23. Ways to make money with free Games:

23.1 In App Purchases:

Game owners get money through the In App Purchases where users make a purchase to get special features and content, for example to unlock more levels, the purchase is made within the app platform provider, that shares some benefits with the developer in the range of 30% in general, the first genre appeared with the release of iOS in 2009 which continued to grow to include many mobile platforms which got involved, we find four types, among them the subscription- based and the auto renewing subscriptions.

The In App Purchases apply to the premium and the Free app or games known as Freemium as well.

Users spend real money this way without realizing it therefore a password is needed before buying any game to protect the owner that shares an iPad or a phone device with another person that could be a child from getting charged for a game he/she didn't buy.

23.2 In game advertising:

Banners, pop-ups are used, and offers to sign up for a service could be a trial or a video to watch and you'll get something, even if the user is not spending money the developer get some money for advertising the info, it is very common, sometimes if you pay you can get rid of the adds.

Usually measured in CPM which stands for Cost per mill (mill means thousand) called CPT (a commercial term) as well, a method of measurement found in advertising, that includes TV, Radio and more.

A division of the advertising cost and the numbers of impressions in thousands meaning cost per 1000.

It is a viable method but not enough.

23.3 IGA: (in-game advertising)

Is a method to monetize your game, it tries to reach 16 to 34 years old male category that uses gaming to relax, it can be static displaying the brand names and profesional products that cannot be changed once programmed into your game, or it can be dynamic, thanks to the internet it is possible as soon as the game is lanched the adds are delivered this way, the IGA is a time sensitive because the adds are out even before the game advertised for is finished.

23.4 Online games Advertisement:

Includes games that you can play the basics online and the Freemium ones, the user gets offers to purchase advanced items, the idea is that users once used to the game and playing for a long time will buy additional features to continue playing.

23.5 Pay to Play:

Where users have to pay to access the game, and sometimes IGA is not included.

24. Targeted Audience:

Avoid assumptions, it is not because you like your game others will do the same, so don't assume that users like it too, you might think that your game is fun, but is it really? Think again, if you found it so don't assume that others will do too.

Don't assume that differentiating between the age categories and between man and women is the way to go, a teenager and a 50 years old might play the same game, and male or female can be attracted to play as well similar games.

Games are played by a big range of age and teenagers are not really a huge market, because they normally don't have too much money to spend on games, patience is needed to play complex games, and that sweets older people.

It is advised to do some research before to design a game to pick your target audience, guessing is not good.

25. Game Statistics:

According to esa's facts (esa: entertainment software association) regarding the game industry, billions of dollars are spent on video games, hardware, and accessories in 2013, 53% accounts for the digital sales type, adds-on content, and networking games, the average player and consumer is in the 30's range, the average age of purchaser is 35 years old, Over 50% of American families own a console game, and almost 50% are women playing games over age of 18 and older that's 36% greater than boys (17%) same age category.

82% of children have their parents permission to either buy or rent a game, 95% of parents check the content before allowing their kids to play believing that games are good impact on their children.

A research stated that 91% of children between age of 2 and 17 play video games, 25% of all gamers are in the age category of over 50 years old.

26. Helping the user:

It is always good to include instructions in your games helping the users to play with ease knowing which keys to press, do not assume all gamers know already which key to press A key, or D, or (W, A, S, D) group for first time game users, you need to guide them and help them, including a brief tutorial is worthed, ask your audience about the game, a pretest with friends and family is the way to start then the audience of course has a view as well, the feedback is critical to make a successful game, finding a similar game to yours is a good way to find out what to include in yours, do not copy but just try that game to get a feel and what users expect from you, translation is critical because games are played by speaking different language, or maybe users cannot even read, so better think about these little things to include, consider also the issue having a game released with offending contents to some users, or too aggressive to play by a certain category, so it is good to avoid all that and focus on quality, picking the right type of game, choosing a nice content, and then communicating it in an easy and simple way, all that helps your game be successful.

You don't have to stress over each country, and each region but try to study important points that help you market your product, think about the big picture and target millions of users.

27. Risks and Challenges:

There are of course risks to be a game developer, cost is one of them, even mentioned earlier that there are tools free to use, the more advanced ones you need to pay for them such as 3D Max, and Photoshop that has great features, also your time invested in the process is money, why not hire someone to make assets for your game therefore save you time ($$$) , there are also fees to pay to publish your game in certain platforms, also find out if the game engine software that you choose to use doesn't have further costs to get your game in the commercial world and if it does find out your licencing fees, some software are free at the beginning then to give you licence and commercial right you need to pay.

It is also overwhelming to be the artist, the programmer, the developer and more so investing your time to do that may take months and years to learn all that, to master all of them it is definitely a long way of experiencing what works and what doesn't, so try to balance between your efforts and time and how much it will cost you, if you outsource the project or parts of it, it is of course up to you to consider what works best for you, learning how to make an asset can take time versus buying it for a simple affordable fee, again assets can be very sophisticated and expensive.

One of the risks as well is you investing efforts, time and money and once the game released it didn't do very well, because users did not enjoy playing it, or because it is not appealing or...could be any reason, So the best to avoid that is Start Small and go from there, by expanding later on by adding more features similar to angry birds game. So releasing small games at a time, finding if users love them then grow.

Many developers experienced already the whole process of releasing and testing their games and finding what works versus what doesn't then over time came up with great games that millions downloaded and played.

Making your fist steps to the game world is exciting and risky but with small steps you will get there.

It is like starting at a junior level for your first job then by learning and then mastering the tools, or standards you become the experienced that knows what is going on and how to fix problems and make things work.

Another advice is to listen to the feedback, pay attention what the majority of users are complaining about and finding frustrating, or if they want more assets in the game, feedback is good to enhance and make a change to your game in a positif way, just release and move to the next steps.

Each game is specific and needs specific changes to make it better, finding the problems and fixing them is definitely the key to go towards success and becoming a good developer.

28. <u>Things To Consider</u>:

Having the designer's critical mind to design a game is very important while developing your game, being able to analyse yourself the game is certainly a positive point, by playing many other games you can develop that ability of criticizing and analyzing your own project to make it more useful, fun, and appealing.

There are many resources to check out to continue learning and advancing for example for game engines Unity has tutorials that you can find on their site.

Be curious and question how assets are made, or a character, so you'll be playing but trying to dig and find the details behind the scene instead of just playing, therefore acting as if you where the designer, find out how much complexity or none he/she went through to make the game, question if other choices were available for the designer? Which strategy or planning the designer followed and did he/she consider pushing the user going a certain direction when playing? Try to take the game apart into pieces to understand how the whole game works all together and by doing so you will know how to construct and design your game.

You have to start somewhere, save a copy of the game and use the tools they are offering you to understand their games, many are open to public offering you a chance to get experience before jumping into making your own games by learning to identify problems if any and solve them.

29. Conclusion:

If you ever wanted to enter the game business, if you ever wanted to make your own games, this book will help you plan ahead by giving you the right tools and the right steps to follow to start.

No worries anymore once you know what to do to jump into this very exiting business.

Do it for fun or choose it as a career the choice is yours!

ACKNOWLEDGMENTS

To You, dear readers for trying to learn
how to be part of the exciting game industry world
and Enter the Game Business!.

www.ingramcontent.com/pod-product-compliance
Lightning Source LLC
Chambersburg PA
CBHW071017180526
45168CB00003B/1457